E PALES 74975

REFERS

HILDA VAUGHAN

POETRY NOW

CENTRAL 1994

Edited by Veronica Hannon

First published in Great Britain in 1994 by
POETRY NOW
1-2 Wainman Road, Woodston,
Peterborough, PE2 7BU

FOREWORD

Although we are a nation of poetry writers we are accused of not reading poetry and not buying poetry books: after many years of listening to the incessant gripes of poetry publishers, I can only assume that the books they publish, in general, are books that most people do not want to read.

Poetry should not be obscure, introverted, and as cryptic as a crossword puzzle: it is the poet's duty to reach out and embrace the world.

The world owes the poet nothing and we should not be expected to dig and delve into a rambling discourse searching for some inner meaning.

The reason we write poetry (and almost all of us do) is because we want to communicate: an ideal; an idea; or a specific feeling. Poetry is as essential in communication, as a letter; a radio; a telephone, and the main criteria for selecting the poems in this anthology is very simple: they communicate.

Faced with hundreds of poems and a limited amount of space, the task of choosing the final poems was difficult and as editor one tries to be as detached as possible (quite often editors can become a barrier in the writer-reader exchange) acting as go between, making the connection, not censoring because of personal taste.

In this anthology over one hundred and sixty poems are presented to the reader for their enjoyment.

The poetry is written on all levels; the simple and the complex both having their own appeal.

The success of this collection, and all previous *Poetry Now* anthologies, relies on the fact that there are as many individual readers as there are writers, and in the diversity of styles and forms there really is something to please, excite, and hopefully, inspire everyone who reads the book.

Contents

Christmas Sonnet

In olden days so it is written
Christmas is a time of love
not courtly love with which one's smitten
but love of Christ from above.
Scribes and sages of present times
say Mammon rules OK!
and Christmas bells and Christmas chimes
are the tills of modern day.
The wise kings who were searching west
following their star so bright
had greater knowledge to divest
of endless love that night.
In Jesus' birth we will proclaim
his Christmas love our true domain.

Colin Pountney

Afterlife Party

Our spirits fly forth in timeless flight
They dance in the garden of eternal light
A galaxy of friends with which to feast
Their souls alive, bodies deceased
A joyous celebration for all to see
The happiness of lovers forever free
Heavenly music, the radiant sun
Emotional bliss, never ending fun
The afterlife party, everlasting wine
Float in the sky, just feeling divine
Don't shed a tear when you draw your last breath
You'll join us here in this wonderful death.

Simon Fenn

Europe 1993

Today I had my eye lashes dyed
Today thirty-five Bosnians died
Yesterday I fed a bottle bank with glass
Yesterday the City felt the glass-shattering blast
Tomorrow I must work then go to bed
Tomorrow, then, will all hope be dead?
Barbara Wood

Wearing Her Gloves

I might have known
they'd come to this
(sodden, stiff, restitched leather
black with age at the fingertips)
for reaching to rescue was always
her natural gesture.

And now, on a pouring Good Friday
wellie-shod, umbrella-sheltered,
I find her gloves take over.

They point towards worms
who in manic lost judgement
launch themselves across tarmac
black and awash, a river of death.
They stretch out in rubbery rings
for the far side, for yielding earth.

The gloves direct my hands
like angels of a saving grace
scooping alarmed loops of life
onto dry palms, to let them spiral
back to a leafy tunnel.

From the great wheel of death
my bidden hands snatch them
turning or lifting each slither of cells.

For our own kind in their agony
of hatred, killing, endless war,
we can do nothing, these gloves and I,
yet here on a bad Friday,
saving these simple creatures
suggests that some time
good may come again?
Janet E Harrison

Greek Dance
Pounding,
memories of a long lost
past,
sense spiralling music
sounds,
feet slapping music
beats,
tunes of a heart now
gone:
always, never, always, never,
there.
Nikos Athanasou

The *'Knead'* for Massage
The Greek name for massage is the word *knead*
Mentioned in 460 BC by Hippocrates.
To treat the whole person is the philosophy
Behind massage, Shiatsu and reflexology.
For anxiety and stress there can be relief
Through meditation in motion, which is known as T'ai - Chi.
Learn yoga to control the body and mind
And get Qi flowing through the Meridian Lines.
The Yin Yang balance must be restored, for good measure,
And the body's healing powers be improved by Acupressure.

There are many ways one can help one's self,
There's the Alexander technique - it improves one's health.
Massage can relax and restore harmony,
Give a feeling of well-being and vitality.
Listen to your hands when you give a massage,
During kneading, friction or effleurage.
Though you give so much, there is a reward,
Through compassion and trust there can be a rapport.
With every massage, or whatever you do,
Trust the unseen hand that will follow you through.
Joyce Simmonds

The Circus
In a field just down the road
The circus men, their tent unload
A massive thing, striped red and white
To see it rise, oh what a sight

Soon the seats are in the marquee
The ring is ready for the matinee
Clowns into their costumes get
With noses red and baggy suit
They look so cheeky and so cute

The horses groomed to look their best
Their plumes and harness looking great
The guys and gals upon the highwire
Putting all their skills to test

Jugglers practice in the ring
One wheel cyclists do their thing
In their cages just outside
Hear the tigers roar with pride

All is ready, the people in
The band its overture begin
All is set, the show can start
The children thrill to every part

There's laughter, thrill, and danger too
Precision timing thro' and thro'
The circus is so great to see
From little child to OAP.
George Emery

For the Night
Whisper meander throughout the world
On twisting crooked winds that curl
Their crooked way below the ducking cloud draped sun;
Twist across the vast dull hues and sounds of grey bedlam.
Curl out upon the day and roll out upon the heath
For the night must come exulting in a quiet breath.

Let the crooked curling wind dole Adam's living whisper low
Death's infirmity shall not be drawn across Eve's hapless brow
And the quiet joyful night shall condole
The bloodshot anguish of Eve's despondent soul.

Let then the dawn roar out upon the heath
But the night must come exulting in a quiet breath.
Denis Lee Combs

A Flower Called Northamptonshire
A land beset with pride and past
That owes much to the cobbler's last
A people unafraid to toil;
To forge a living from its soil
America's star spangled banner
Flies high outside of Sulgrave Manor
Reminding people living near:
Washington's forebears once lived here
Standing against industrial sprawl,
The ghostly remains of Kirby Hall

A palace that was once so grand
Is now an empty wonderland
Unlike the Hall of Cottesbrooke
Where heritage lovers come to look
At beauty that is proudly shown
Outside the house of brick and stone
Intrigue of history arouses
Interest in these country houses
Each aligned to distant spires
In this county: Rose of the Shires.
Alan Marston

Purse Strings
I does me shopping daily
Instead of once a week,
I haves to make me pension last
By buying things that's cheap.

I don't buy fancy cakes and such,
Or steaks, or chops, or salmon;
Streaky bacon takes the place
Of a nice big slice of gammon!

Instead of beef on Sunday
Its sausages in my pud,
Yes, I still haves me Yorkshire,
And it still tastes just as good!

Toad-in-the-hole they call it
It's such a funny name;
But still it's very tasty
And it feeds me just the same.

To think that when to work I went
I never worried what I spent!
Money all too easy came
I ought to hang my head in shame.

We never learn, till it's too late,
The folly of our destined fate;
The future years that lie ahead,
Old age is something young ones' dread.

But now it's here, it's not so bad,
I think of all the things I've had,
Lots of good times, loads of fun
I wouldn't swop with anyone!
Joan C Cook

Knickers!
'Are yu cumin' aaaat tu play?'
You asked my child within
And she was dying to, that day
But the elastic snapped in her knicker leg -
me baggy green uns -
And she didn't have a'ssertafety pin!
Maggie Bowler

Looking Out on a Summer Evening
Look out.
What do I see?
I see people looking
But they can't see me.

I see the wheelbarrow,
Watering can and swing.
I can hear them playing
But they can't hear me.

For my breathing is quiet,
As quiet as can be.
I can hear and see them
But they don't know I'm here.
Zoë Smith (7)

Women

Our own worst enemies
From the first, our mother
Who bade us to fly
And pushed back the clouds
Yet bashed a peg of recriminations
Into the ground
To keep us from getting too far.
Donna Vizma

The Lonely Soldier

A lonely soldier on the battlefield
Not like the old days with sword and shield
Guns are blazing and bullets fly
And all around his friends they die.

He wonders why he is sitting here?
As his heart begins to beat with fear
He thinks of his family and starts to cry
This lonely soldier just a boy.

He does his duty he takes a stand
To serve his country to save his land
Never to wonder to do or die
This lonely soldier just a boy.
Brian Anthony Smyth

Consolation

Her husband doesn't love her,
She is quite convinced of that.
Her eyes are full of unshed tears,
As she eats a chocolate.

Her husband doesn't love her,
And he hates her being fat,
She promises she'll try to diet,
But she eats a chocolate.

Her husband doesn't love her,
She strokes her old grey cat,
A tear begins to fall,
So she eats a chocolate.
Christine Pearce

Villanelle
I will make sure your company is mine.
Even for a few hours every week.
My ecstasy is brief, but so divine.

Your smile, your laugh, the way you neglect time
Make me a trembling female, oh, so weak!
I will make sure your company is mine.

Spurn me not, I'll be a clinging vine
Should you decide our love has reached its peak.
My ecstasy is brief, but so divine.

My letters you return, yet line by line
You break my heart. Your ire has reached its peak.
My ecstasy is brief, but so divine.

Even for a few hours every week
Should you decide our love has reached its peak,
I will make sure your company is mine,
My ecstasy is brief, but *so* divine.
Marion Brown

Nostalgia
Lace curtains
Sighing in the autumn wind -
Memories stir.

Spring showers
Creep softly over open fields -
Fresh love.

A summer shared
Intensified the heat
Of young love.

Autumn leaves, once green
Now brown - we too
Grow old.

A lone skater
On the ice-clad lake -
Heartbreak.

The curtains close -
The mind blots out
All bitterness.
Mary Slaymaker

My Teddy Bear
I have a little furry friend,
He's called a teddy bear,
He lives with me in my house,
Comes with me everywhere.

When I sit at the table,
My friend is always there,
His place is there beside me,
On my little wooden chair.

He doesn't wear much clothing,
'cause he has a coat of fur,
I'm sure he's warm in summer,
But in winter he goes *Brr.*

I take him in the garden,
So he can watch me play,
He sits just where I put him,
And never runs away.

I take him up to bed with me,
When I lay down to sleep,
To make sure he's still with me
Sometimes I have a peep.
Angela Constable

I Wonder . . .
I wonder if exits are on the way out.
I wonder if juggling is catching
I wonder if anger will be all the rage.
I wonder if there's another word for thesaurus.
Lesley Beevers

Compassion
Her long arms extend
Embracing children, women, men.
She is there in the dry air
Of the Indian summer
Spilling hot tears over the crushed bodies
Buried in an earthquake's wrath.
She has seen it all before, the dead
Lying among the ruins of a bombed city.
She has cradled the bodies of airmen
Falling from an exploding aircraft
On a moonless night.

She is the last kiss on a cold white cheek
And the hand that reaches out
To touch those who are left and mourn.
Vivien Bayley

Then - and Now

The farm house ruined and forlorn -
Dutch barn empty, its roof wind torn,
the byre is bare, the yards are still,
birds flutter over the windowsill.

The slates are gone, the walls awry,
the garden's lost, the weeds waist high,
the gate is off, the rafters rot,
the floors have cracked and sunk a lot.

It is so sad to see it now,
I can remember clearly how
a family lived within these walls
and cattle fattened in the stalls.

Some children played around the yard,
a dog would chase me - barking hard,
the barn was filled with baled hay,
always something to watch each day.

In nineteen-ninety-two I found
the place had been razed to the ground,
of house and barn or yard - no trace,
just two wire strands around the place.

The loading ramp across the track
weed covered - and with broken back,
the only thing that I could see
of the place as it used to be.

In words and pictures now I strive
to keep those memories alive
of holidays and schoolboy fun
in harvest fields and summer sun.

Philip Jenkins

Untitled

I look into your eyes,
I feel
a soft veil of emotion
envelop me.
You touch your flesh
against mine.
I feel a warmth
with hidden depth,
that thaws
my frozen heart.
Your breath kindles
a long forgotten fire,
that was once an ember
I called my soul.
I look at you
and for a time
I am complete.
Paul T Millett

You Were on My Mind

(Dedicated to my daughter Karen on her birthday, December 31)

You were on my mind when I woke up this morning
And I've been thinking about you all day.
Remembering your smile, your voice, the sound of your laughter,
Remembering little things we shared,
Wondering how long it will be before we're together again,
With time to share even more.
I can't think of anyone or anything but you today
I guess that means I'm missing you even more than I usually do.
Grace Bexon

From Peter Newcombe's Water Colour Snowdrops
Silver and grey shadows there
stretched across fields as
voices breathe in freezing air.
Snowdrops break from their grave,
struggle through blanket white crystalline,
the bramble, not winter's slave
raises its long arm - intertwine.

The artist's brush rests, fingers
cold, sketch partially finished,
as slate blue sky lingers,
foreground predominantly clear,
subtle colours sublime and rare
winter reeds, village and church here
arrested in a grey-silver lair.
Rob Kendall

Colours of Autumn
Crimson the carpet,
Golden the leaves,
Drooping, swaying,
Goes the old oak tree.

There flies the swallow,
Off for her journey.

Sky is dull, ever so lonely.
Sly is the fox, through the trees.

Hibernated ladybirds as well as bees.
Peck goes the blackbird on frosty ground.
Golden leaves to be found.
Anna Simmonds (9)

Why?

Why in summer are the poppies red
as they grace the fields of corn?
Why do the birds in chorus sing
at the breaking of each dawn?
The sky now, why is it, oh! so blue
and white clouds wear a pinkish hue?
Why do the children in summer array
love to get out on a warm, bright day?
They skip and they jump to show their delight,
Some run, some walk, some ride a bike,
Times have changed, aye, that is true,
But we all salute summer when winter is thro'.

Betty Daley

Nine Months

I see her
Dancing naked underneath the moonlight,
her belly swollen yet still she dances - elegantly.
Her long, brown hair covers her swollen, milky breasts.
Uninhibited - she dances.
Her hands in the air exposing her vulnerable child-to-be.
As I watch her, it moves me,
to see this naturally deformed body seem so beautiful.
It moves me . . .
But wait. I am looking into water.
It's me - I see myself.

Lucy Pearce

Winter's Child

What is this April, this stunted, changeling child
of winter, this rain-soaked span of nature's year.
Caught between the bitterness of age and sweetness
of youth, the cold of nights passing and the
warmth of dawns to come, you hang suspended and
uncertain, await the opening of the bud, the sun
upon your back.

But slowly first, then with a silent rush
set out nature's wares upon a field of green.
The whispering has ceased, and with bold shout
proclaim the circle has been joined at last
and summer's here again.
Robert M

Bozeat

If you are a lady with oversize feet.
You are sent over to Bozeat.
For there they do not stare.
Every lady has got big feet everywhere.
For a lady with big feet
This must be quite sweet.
Jason Smith

Catkins

In the gully with the water
Lies the debris of our lives,
Cans and papers and plastic things
That we love to throw away.
But soaring above all this I saw
A cloud of golden catkins
Dancing in the wind.
Winifred Amey Richardson

A Nice Cup of Darjeeling Tea With Two Brown Sugars (raw cane) and Soya Milk (non-animal produce)

I honestly can't think of a single time in my life
I wouldn't gladly exchange for five minutes with you.
Your Tarot cards say I'm no good for you,
even the hamster issues ultimatums,
but the girl in the health food shop understands.
Richard Jeary

Springtime

Lovely spring,
Wonderful spring,
Pretty buds opening
And the birds sing.
New life is born everywhere around,
Flowers of all colours, grow from the ground.

Sunshine's rays,
Brighten our days,
Giving joy in our hearts,
For this we give praise.
Frisky lambs skipping and jumping with glee,
The soft green grass, so refreshing to see.

A little bird's nest,
Where the tiny ones rest,
Parent birds feeding them,
With increasing zest,
Lily leaves floating on the top of the pool,
Where the sunbeams dancing, meet the waters cool.

Nightingales singing,
Their trilling notes ringing,
Through woodland foliage,
Sweet notes to us bringing.
Sunshine and shadow through the green leaves,
Giving such a beautiful picture to please.

Billows foaming white,
Like horses in flight,
Constantly moving,
Even in the moonlight,
The waves reflecting the blue of the sky,
Or the grey and the white of the clouds floating by.

Golden daffodils,
With their trumpet frills,
God's mystic beauty,
Our wondering heart fills.
His is the glory of all things that we see,
Our god and creator, heaven's reality.

The moon shining bright,
Through the dark of the night,
Reflecting the glory,
Of the sunshine's light.
And the twinkling stars which are always there,
But in the sun's radiance, they seem to disappear.

God's glorious earth
And the wonders of birth,
Our every experience,
Of sorrow and mirth,
The wonderful reality of His great love,
And his constant presence, from heaven above.

Earth's spring will not stay,
It will soon pass away,
But the love of Jesus,
Brings heaven's glorious day,
A kingdom where nothing will fade, and die,
We shall see the dear Saviour, who loves you and I.

Flowers will not fade,
In the heavenly glade,
No sorrow, or death,
In heaven's restful shade,
No partings will be there forevermore,
But God's love, joy, and peace, on heaven's shore.
Doris L Middleditch

Live the Hard Truth
about love, drag shit-stained sheets
from her bed. Wipe spittle slack lips,
comb matted hair and cut
yellowed fingernails that scar
sodden skin. Your hands

lift brittle bone and thready muscle,
sponge soiled buttocks, rinse puke
from favourite night-gowns and hang,
empty outside Emergency
at three am. Fingers

see far more than eyes, cradle
a heart hammered old, cover
the cold edge of death. Tilt the pot,
tea trembles into your cup, spills,
every shiver of your hand.
K V Skene

Wassit Like?
Wassit like bein' an' old black man,
drinkin' tea from an old tin can?
Wassit like at the bottom of the class,
gettin' the blame an' a kick up the arse ?

Wassit like in a tower block flat,
or goin' for a walk in a Rasta hat?
Wassit like if you marry a white
when your face is black like the dead of night?

Wassit like livin' on the dole
in a ghetto town run down hole?
Wassit like takin' the blame
for why life in England ain't the same?
Robert Cook

The Plan

The Lord himself descended, shapened as man,
He came as our redeemer, to fulfil the perfect plan,
The plan that wrought redemption -
Through divine thought and word,
The plan that brought salvation,
Through the voice that would be heard.
As one, 'Crying in the wilderness,' -
The lamb of God was slain,
'Twas you and I beloved,
Who caused that heartfelt pain.
For you and I, that Jesus,
The awful winepress trod,
That we should have atonement with the one and triune God.
Ruth E Kenworthy

The Saturday Children

I can collect at ten from
the house I called home
to be allowed the company of
and renew an acquaintance
with my own children
for set hours.

I'm dad one greeted by the
man who knows more from
and about living with my
daughter and son than I do now.
They, taught disposable
relationships, learnt
quickly not to cry
but I never did.

Soon my new lady will share
our sixth day trips. Another
mother, but try to love her.
Must be back by four, when
I leave these parts
of myself at the door.
Sally Angell

Sky

Just by looking at the sky above
You'll see the sweetness of my love.
If the sky is dull and grey
I pine for you so far away.
If the sky is ruled by snow or rain
I need to see you smile again.
If the sky is turmoiled by wind or storm
I need you to keep me safe and warm.
If sunset or rainbow colour the sky
I somehow feel that you are nigh.
If the clouds are fluffy and white
I am longing to hold you tight.
If black clouds are all you see
I need you to rescue me.
If the sky glitters with the stars and moon
You know that I will see you soon.
But if the sky is just plain blue
Just remember that I love you.
Vivien Mary Phillips (16)

British Weather

It's a strange old saying, 'There's a nip in the air,'
If you look all around, can you see it there?
Then after a while it bites at your nose
And quickly runs down to your fingers and toes
You still cannot see it, but you know it's still there
So next time you're out you'd better *beware*!

After a while you anticipate the chill
And you wrap up warm of your own free will
Out you go all covered and cosy
but your hands are hot and your cheeks get rosy
Everyone else is as surprised as you
Summer's sneaked back and, nobody knew.
Sarah Lilly

Thinking Englandly and New Englandly
From the Old World of sonnets and ironies
buttoned up in this straight jacket of Form
come seeking new air, new Eden - some warm
thawing out of English proprieties.
Sixteen twenty to nineteen eighty eight:
the Pilgrim Fathers play computers now
Calvin, Thrift, the Day of Judgement allow
today's Bostonian excess Worldly Weight.
Oh! Emily! what would you say? I came
here for your batty visions - loaded gun -
I came for the obliquities of your soul.
Now I know why your queasy quatrains frame
your pain. You - couldn't - even - have - begun
to meet Christ lover in your nervous role.

Lowell?
Ti Jean turns Beat Kerouac and off I launch on a
crazy bebop trip out West 100 mph in battered
car over Rocky Mountain Pass into purple sunset
unholy haze of booze, girls, blues . . . a wild orgy
of infantile self . . . my American Dream . . .

No
What may flower has been deflowered.
It'll be back to the Old World of sonnets and ironies.
Mark Floyer

winter deckchairs
you can't see what's not
worth seeing
what's face in your face
down your throat like a fog
there is
nothing O ordinariness
the mundane

scratching around for
a truth
when there just isn't one

there are walls
but not doors
a love of surfaces
has left me wanting

the thaw arrived too late
an offered branch
whitened with waiting

it was real enough
and meant nothing

I could be accelerating
through marshmallow
for the rest of my life

the call of the tame
Sarah Wood

Echoes
I heard it as the morning breeze
Bore it through the rustling trees
And o'er the restless, sobbing seas
'I'll wait for you, my darling.'

It fell upon my inner ear
The sound I thought no more to hear
The tones I always held so dear
The voice of my lost darling.

And then I heard it on the rain
That beat upon my window pane
It called again and yet again
'Come to me, my darling.'

The lonely years so soon will be
No more than just a memory
And I, forever more shall be
United with my darling.
Katherine Chew

The True Story of Davy Jones
I can tell 'ee stories, son, true stories of the sea
For I knowed Davy Jones, my boy, an' Davy Jones knowed me
We sailed the China Seas, ol' son, through the Penang Straits,
Davy Jones an' me, me boy, 'im an' me was mates.

At nights I dreams of Davy Jones, an' them places what we saw
An sailin' them ol' clipper ships at a dozen knots an' more
I 'ears the ol' sea shanties, on the moanin' evein' breeze
That Davy Jones an' me once sung, as we sailed them China Seas

Poor Davy liked 'is grog, me boy, an' Davy drank 'is fill
In the bilges there they found 'im, lying cold an' still
so we stitched 'im in a canvas, with 'is bottle in 'is 'and
And Davy Jones went overboard, a thousand miles from land

I saw Davy off, my boy, 'twas in the China Sea
'e woke up before 'e sank, an' waved goodbye to me
'appy, smilin' Davy Jones, I 'eard 'is farewell call
'I'm not dead, you stupid sod - I'm only drunk, yer fool'

Now 'e's sittin' on 'is locker, one thousan' fathom deep
An' 'e welcomes all you sailor men, to everlastin' sleep
To everlastin' sleep, me lad, somewheres to rest your bones
The final port of call, ol' son, down there with Davy Jones

An' when your time is up, me boy, 'e'll greet you as a brother
A glass of grog in 'is right 'and, a bottle in the other
so when you sees ol' Davy Jones, when the bugles sound
Tell 'im, boy, 'Yer get 'em in,' 'is turn to buy the round

So 'ere's to Davy Jones, me son, an' the stirring tale I've told,
I'll 'ave a drop of Nelson's blood, it 'elps keep out the cold
Every word was true, me boy - would I tell you a lie?
Let's 'ave another noggin then, afore yer says goodbye
Ronald Ellis

Golden Eagle in Scotland
Rocks swell about us now;
Bleak, lofty, rugged ground.
We deftly continue.
Awesome soar we glimpse,
Dark wing span convinced:
One young eagle flew.
M J Hopkins

Geriatric
Sometimes, you peep out from behind the bushes of Fantasy
To pick the fragrant flowers of Memory
And offer them, smiling, to me.

You skip lightly down the steps of Then
And run across the sunny lawns of When.
You dip your fingers in the pool of Ability
And lift your face to the warm rays of
How it Used To Be.

Then you rest upon the seat of Oh So Long Ago
And listen to the birds singing All You Used To Know.
Oh, how the fountains of your Early Years
Sparkle in the sun,
As unchecked glisten my tears,
When I see what Age has done.

The orchard hangs heavy with the fruits of Remembering,
But some fall and are bruised before their gathering,
And the lovely garden of your mind
Is tangled and overgrown
With the choking weeds of Confusion
And of Being Alone.

But the rusted gates of Now are no barrier to you
As effortlessly you slip through
And make your escape,
Back to the landscape of Sensibility
And the sweet, blossoming Parkland of
Once This Was Me.
Iris Gertrude Bell

Northampton Castle
Four hundred years ago the castle stood
Rust brown and massive by the river Nene
Dank and decaying, it was ancient then
It's loathsome dungeons stained by Saxon blood.

Expediency made a just award
The sullen citizens in vengeful mood
Committed Senlis and his swarthy brood
To haunt the precincts of a railway yard.

For me there breathes a baleful atmosphere
This bloody spot cannot buy time alone
For countless years of tyranny atone
Nor cleansing winds disperse the scent of fear.

Only one russet monument remains
A buttressed postern in a crumbling wall
Destined to purge the guilt of vanished Gaul
Trembling obeisance to the passing trains.
Herbert Waddilove Hircock

A View to the Future
These things are immaterial
All that matters is you
You must live any way you can
Fighting is no longer a sport
It has become a way of life
Computers doing everything
Everybody has been programmed
Staying alive is the aim
Only the toughest will survive.
There is no longer any love in this world
Peace and harmony are just useless words
Human beings have no feelings
They just wander through life
Staggering across the years
Chains bind the children
Killing now a national sport
A blood chilling look at the future
Or the way we live today?
Tracy E Payne

I'm Not Going Bald
Staring in the mirror
I'm confused at what I see
That face staring back
Doesn't quite look like me

There's something wrong, I know there is
As I look and stare
Then I realise with a shock
That I've got no hair

I'm not going bald
I've still got one hair on my head
I'm not going bald
That's right, that's what I said

A funny thing happened
As I screamed at my loss
What the hell was I going to do
With no hair on my bonce?

At the barbers the other day
I had sat down in a chair
I felt the snip of scissors around my head
That must be where I lost my hair

Then I sat up and did some thinking
At what my loss had done
It had saved me getting dandruff
And my head felt as smooth as my bum

So whether it's alopecia
Or a barber that's just gone mad
The thing I'll benefit with no hair
May not be all that bad

John David Whitaker

Liberty

I seem to stand here,
and dance to entertain a crowd
that ignores me.
Do they think I enjoy doing this?
And when everyone leaves,
I too will go.
But not to a home full of warmth,
full of love and contentment.
But to a cage that is too small for me,
and to a place
too small for humanity.

Caroline Maughan

Crowning Glory

That woman's crowning glory is her hair
Is sometimes just a statement of despair;
That splendid bouffant that you so admire
Is seldom but acquired without tire.

With damp dejected locks she often sits
While little stands are parted, and the bits
Onto a plastic porcupine are stuck,
Twisted around, secured by metal hook.

Uncomfortably the process thus continues
Until the whole head bristles like the sinews
Of pale pink rolls of porcupinal prickle.
Even the ears suffer under the stickle
And beg to be released before they're torn -
They feel just like the cow with crumpled horn.

At last the process finished, the next stage
Is being dried inside a sort of cage
That looks as if it came from outer space,
That hums and deafens all, without a trace
Of finer feelings. But now all is dry,
With what relief, and with what a wry
Smile those porcupinal tortures can be shed.
A few deft strokes of brush and comb ahead;
Then with what joy to view the finished state -
The artist's full reward for all the hate.
Ella Edwards

Skinhead Ballerina

naked in Hatfield you dance
flirting with life and simplicity
through passions ignored
by the way we live now

the call of the eye
a kiss in the shrug of the shoulder
turning and coaxing
tossing rejecting you bound
through space and through time
stopping gently for moments
of touch or encounter
physical and certain
powerful movements
set off in the glitter of gesture
the tension has turned
from the tight frightened face
I remember
for now you are telling a story
of joy of engagement
stripped of concerns inhibitions
the burden of problems
the daft masquerades
of our costumes
Susee Magenta

Girlfriend

With eyes of green,
That I think brown,
So kind, yet proud,
With depth to drown.

That glint of spark,
Your pretty laugh,
So sweetly coy,
When you feel daft.

To break that shell was tough enough,
But from it grew the strongest tree,
Its blossom our undying love,
The fruit a smile from you to me.

That pout of lip,
So quick to quip,
With eyes ablaze
And hands on hip.

And all is shared,
Our souls are bare,
Friends that care,
I'll always be there.

For if you search inside and seek,
You'll find a piece of me there too,
This soul of mine is yours to keep,
A joy to say that I love you.

Adam Sparshott

Reflections

Still water 'neath a shady tree,
Where I can sit in calm tranquillity,
With just my thoughts to keep me company,
To let my heart and soul roam free.

I feel the sunshine warm upon my face,
As clouds glide overhead with gentle pace,
A butterfly floats by with fragile grace,
Whilst Dragonflies dart thither place to place.

The busy bees sip nectar from the flowers,
In lush grass green and fresh from summer showers,
Where Oak and Poplar stand like stately towers
And bird song fills the warm and sunny hours.

The bouquet from the flowers fills the air,
With honeysuckle, garlic, rose and tare,
The poppy, cornflower, sage and daisy fair,
Their perfume heady, sweet beyond compare.

A Lark on high, her joyful song doth sing,
As swallows dip and wheel on agile wing,
Whilst distant bells from yonder church do ring,
Their message one of hope for all to bring.

I thank the Lord who gave these things to me,
With ears to hear and eyes that I might see,
The trees, the flowers, the creatures wild and free,
Life's treasures cherished always, in my memory.
Jackie Barlow

R I P - (Oh! Surrey Vale)

Meadow Vale in garland green
Danced to the beat of the
tambourine

Meadow Vale in golden gown
Waltzed and sighed
As the leaves drift down

Meadow Vale
On a cold cold day
Died in the path of
A motorway.
Teresa White

From a Hotel Bedroom at Night

Female squeals, male bellows
Echo down the canyons of the night,
Dissipate.
Suzuki's rev and roar like drums,
Reverberate.
Lonely gulls proclaim their rights,
Disconsolate.

Day words compel within my head,
Unwholesome trait.
Let go. Then silence.
Dissociate.
Joyce Crewe

Oh Fabled Pontrhydyfen . . .

As the mist becomes risen, and the moming dew, glistens upon this monumental land. If you listen, intently, you can hear the valiant echoes that once, and, still do, incarnate, within the vale.
As the stream, gently, glides on momentous past. So begins, another day, in Fabled Pontrhydyfen . . .
David Miles

The Time

It's 10.04 and somewhere a household
celebrity draws a vein and gets ready
to shoot.

It's 10.04 and somewhere a young girl
called Alice is scared her daddy will
come and say goodnight.

It's 10.04 and someone's grandfather is
getting ready to sleep, with a cardboard
blanket and a neon pillow.

It's 10.04 and somewhere a boy was too
embarrassed to buy a condom.

It's 10.04 and I am sitting breaking a
five year oath, never to drink alone.

It's 10.36 and in ten hours the world
will be too embarrassed to mourn their
favourite junkie game show host.

It's 10.36 and Alice lays in a pool of
blood and cum, feeling confused,
scared and betrayed. While her daddy
awaits his two hundred and sixth
hangover of the year.

Its 10.36 and someone's grandfather
lays cold and alone, waiting for the
police to find him and tag his toe with
the infamous Pseudonym John Doe.

It's 10.36 and a young girl lays
sleeping, innocent to the fact
her boyfriends infidelity just
killed her.

It's 10.36 and I sit drinking down
the last shards of a broken oath,
drowning in my own self pity and
I don't give a shit.
I P Atheos

Summer's End
Sparkling web in mornings light.
Nut and bramble, hedgerow ripe.
Bends the bough of apple mellow.
Waves the corn, now golden yellow.

The bonfire bright with fallen leaves
And swallows leave from 'neath the eaves.
Mists across the valley lie.
Summer's end is almost nigh.
Marian Edwards

Night Fishing
The sun sets in the western sky,
Bringing the dusk once more
To mask the flowing tide
As they stand by the shore.

It seems both strange and sorrowful
That they don't give a thought
To the suffering of the fish
Which give them an evening's sport.

But each man is an angler keen
With lamp, with rod, with bait.
They cast into the rolling surf
Their lines with hooks, and wait.

Wait for the noble silver bass,
For mullet and for ray
To take their bait so trustingly
Then they their trust betray.

As they carry home their catch,
The objects of their game,
Should they lose a little pride
And find a little shame?
Arthur Farrington

A W Gamage High Holborn E C 1
Now there's a name to conjure with!
Now there's a thing to tell.
Far, beyond Leather Lane and Seven Dials
It cast a magic spell.
An emporium beyond compare, a feast of expectation
An architectural fantasy, beyond imagination.
Up the shining marble steps, under the towering pediment
In and out of swinging doors, eager shoppers came and went.

Within the massive entrance hall resides a showcase tall and grand.
Put a penny in the slot, and watch toy soldiers,
marching, playing music in the band.
Christmas: Up to the toy department - second floor, ding!
Lies a treasure house beyond compare,
In a grotto Santa sits, what secret thoughts will you declare?
Money flies above your head, by wheels and wires and hissing sounds.
In brass containers, farthings, pennies, ten bob notes and white five pounds.
Down balustraded stairways bronze, past silks and fabrics, plush and fine.
Thro' household goods to bargain basement, a fabled subterranean mine!
Then! blue macaws, and monkeys screech,
Fish and lizards! is it a Zoo?
A cup of tea in the pet department with grey parakeets and love birds too.
Crash! Clash! reticulated gates, now seal the shaft that upwards soars:
Where layered sundries, wares and gifts were heaped in mountains on the floors.
High Holborn's Queen, a jewel, lost.
Was Gamages thro' reign resplendent.
Now ascended to the highest floor,
With Mrs Teal the Lift Attendant.
John A Lampert

Untitled

The hands are old and gnarled now,
yet once they were soft and smooth,
caressing a lover and holding a child secure,
The mouth is slack and weak now,
yet once it was full and firm,
speaking endearments and making joyous sounds.
The eyes are dull and empty now,
yet once they were clear and bright,
promising rapture and filled with compassion.

The head is bent and low now,
yet once it was held up high,
full of pride and confidence in the future.
The span of life is but a moment in time,
and yet it can be the history of tomorrow.
Audrey Donnelly

The Farmer's Lament
I loved the way you drove my plough
You kept it going, I don't know how
You chewed the cud with measured jaw
You knew I had but little straw
And so you made the fodder last
And got the work done very fast
I loved the sweep of your huge horns
I loved you trampling down my corn
I loved the way you made the udders
Of my cows begin to shudder
I wish you'd never caught the pox
I loved you like no other ox.
Paul B Edwards

Nichola's Only Sleeping
I can see her
lying there
gentle pleasant breathing
her limp and lucid arm
announcing her leaving
falling asleep again

Nichola's stockings
covering Nichola's toes
now she's been gone for a while
Nichola's shoes
fall off at the news
Nichola's drunk again

Nichola's time
is free on the mind
hypnotised again
now she is free
as free as her body
Nichola's gone again

She does not mind
if her eyes cannot see
in a whirl for so long
good little brother
which a blanket I smother
Nichola's tucked up for the night
Chris Gregory

Hollow Eyes

You
tortured my soul
with your hollow eyes
when
you looked at me
so far away
your hunger and thirst
your despair
eft me
eeling inadequate
a I
scure
wel fed
felt much sadness at your plight
yet elpless in my armchair
whil you
brused away a fly
from our weeping lips.
Grant Meaby

Ashes to Ashes

Ashes to ashes,
Dust to dust,
Motor car smashes,
All happen to us.

From the beginning,
We live to die
And the beginning,
Is a babies cry.

As we grow older,
More often than not,
Getting much bolder,
To fall from our cot.

On we grow,
Time passes by
And we all know,
That time does fly.

It's coming near,
We have to sigh,
The thing we fear,
Which is to die.

When it's all over,
We will have found,
A field of clover,
Covering a small mound.

Life is all the same,
Didn't you know?
From dust we came
And to dust we shall go.
Terry Friend

The Interview
I woke up in a panic on this auspicious morning
I usually lie and cogitate between my bouts of yawing

But today my palms were sweaty and my heart began to race
As I realised the importance of the task I had to face

I've really got to prove myself and make a strong impression
Be articulate and lucid and gain their full attention

My one and only suit has been cleaned and duly pressed
You should be well presented - a point that's always stressed!

I've made so many applications for employment of some kind
I was prepared to try my hand at any offer I could find

At last I'm on the short list for a Local Government position
I just hope today is favourable and they make the right decision

It would give me such great pleasure, and make my life much better
To join the ranks of the gainfully employed, as a qualified
Refuse Collector!

Ursula Fisher

Unemployment
Lazy days
Going crazy days
Days when I can't afford to eat
Days when I've blisters on my feet
Footslogging days.

Boring days
No-more-ing days
Days when I cannot try to find
Reasons to stimulate my mind
Wasted days.

Endless days
Friendless days
Most of my pals are still in bed
Bank accounts are in the red
What's the point of trying days.

Red letter days
The postman's feet beat out a song
The letter I've waited for so long
The news I thought would never come
Work once more-ing days.
G D McKee

Mother's Day Peace
Clutches of daffodils
Whispers on stairs,
Tea slopped in saucers
Cornflakes and eclairs.

Hushed squeals from the kitchen,
The toaster's alight,
Dad's doing his bit
He's making it right.

Door bounces open
Eyes all aglow,
Tray laden with goodies,
For *Mum's Day* you know.

This is *Her Special Sunday*
You stay there and rest
She'll probably need it
To clean up the mess.
Margaret Allen

Suicide Ledge
Scenes change
Nothing's permanent
Says the girl on the edge of the window ledge

Everybody watching?
Everybody watching?
Shouts the girl on the edge of the suicide ledge

Here goes nothing
In fact, here goes everything
In her mind, muted and blind

She steps off and falls
And bounces the wall
For dismount, four out of ten

Silence for the golden girl
Then screams all around
As nervous blood reddens the ground

Why did she do it?
Why did she do it here?
Surely the coffee wasn't that bad

She wanted to get in early
'Cause the ledge will soon be full
There's a queue forming to bounce the wall.
Mark Norris

Poetry
What do you get from poetry?
Do you like to read it
Or try to write it?
Does that last line evade you
Or does it stick in your mind?

Have you ever thought
How much there must be
Floating about in the world?
Solomon, with five hundred *wives*
Still had time to write it
For some cultures two lines
Is enough to set the mind working
And extending their meaning
Just for yourself - for you
Must be the one
For whom it was written
Lionel Day

Peace of the Seas
O God, protector and navigator of this wild world,
guide me safely through the rough seas of the night
and bring me to lands afar,
for all my faith lies within you for ever more,
If I should die before I reach the countries of the west,
I pray you leave me rest
to sail forever on the ocean's breast,
and as the ghost of my soul sails on and on
on a heavenly ship
but, I shall still feel that rocking, rocking
like a heavenly crib.
Cassandra Doran Jones

The Doll's House Enigma
You sabotaged my doll's house
You played until it broke
Not a tear was given
No apologies were spoke
The doll's house was my lifeline

But you wouldn't comprehend
And now it's smashed to pieces
I don't ever think it'll mend
I know you didn't care for it
It wasn't your concern
But to throw it on the fire
And slowly watch it burn
Was a wicked thing to render?
Was a wicked thought you know?
I'm sure that you have feelings
You just never let them show
Why are you so dogmatic?
Why do you want to see me hurt?
Why am I trodden underfoot
Like unimportant dirt?
The doll's house was my dower
But handed back by you
And now it's ruined beyond repair
So I'll have to start anew
At night I see the doll's house
It comes within a dream
The doll's house is my empty heart
And forever it shall be.
Jim Scavello

Country Memories
A walk in the country was a feast for the eyes
Round every corner a wondrous surprise
Fields of buttercups, so yellow and bright
Intermingled with poppies, a beautiful sight.

The woods full of bells of such intense blue
Turn the world upside down with their fantastic hue
Carpeting the ground, till it looked like the sky
With fragrance more potent than perfume you buy.

The daisies that grew on my father's lawn
We made into necklaces, many a neck to adorn
But I remember most clearly, of all growing wild
The cowslips were my favourite when I was a child
Their tiny creamy flower with leaves soft and green
These are the fond memories of my childhood scene.
Beryl Miles

Love
Love, like a word, can be special.
Love, like a thought, can be kind.
Love, can be heaven,
eternal yet blind.
Love, like a smile, is uplifting.
Love, is a promise unbroken,
with no truer word spoken.
Love is a feeling,
love is a state,
understand its meaning,
before it's too late,
for love is beautiful,
Love is all,
love leaves you standing tall.
Nicolina Manfredi

Mother
They strutted, puffed up, virile
greedy group in a narrow room
flocking like starlings,
plumage darkening
the day.

Glossy black funeral feathers.
Adult males voraciously pecked,
females sober beaked
in black hats fluttered,
bustled.

Sturnus vulgar - is.
Five fleshy claws throbbing with life
extended a coin
silver in the light.
- Go, play.

Small girl's hand a decade old
clutching her lifetime's experience
slapped the insulting coin
cracked the air like bone
scattered the silver piece
silenced the chattering flock
in shock.

Play? - at my Mother's funeral?
Dorothy Ryan

Evening at Sea
Navy blue clouds, heavy, daunting.
Weighing down on an evening sea,
Moving, rolling, with a will of her own,
Unable to be controlled by me.

The beauty of the wildness within her,
The power inherent, not obviously,
Makes me both wondrous and frightened.
Yet called to some place nervously.

I am apart, but yet at one,
Pulled in nature's transfixed gaze,
The green of the horizon, with shaded hue.
Hold my heart gently, I'm trusting in you,
The night descends, as ever, the evening is gone.
Karen Cromer

The Day the Seashells Smiled

Brought akin to nature
By the cackle of twigs amidst burning embers.
My thoughts speed to leafy woodland,
Rustic trees with flowing members.

Deep reds and russet browns
Playing tricks in glints of sunlight
As rays trickle through these wondrous hues
Making dappled patterns on the ground.

Unbroken swathes of bluebells
Stretch for miles round clustering glens.
A definite stillness quells disturbing thoughts
Of mundane modes of living.

Curled beside you now
All trouble seems rosy tinted.
My life seems secure - enveloped
By cosy warmth emanating from the grate.

Chords strung in mutual harmony,
Twin curly mops entwined.
Silky skin drowned in copper pools,
Lips gently brushing mine.

My thoughts return to the morn
And our stroll along the beach.
Where hand in hand we spoke in silence
And calm overrode tide's furore.

Grassy banks undulating to and fro
Due to the tumult of the breeze
Which caught crimson vitality on our cheeks;
A couple relishing in their love.

Together we admired the heady cliffs,
Pausing to explore each crag.
We marvelled at our creation,
In awe of the inky blue around.

And when your eyes looked down into mine
And you asked me to be yours,
Every grain of sand had significance,
Each seashell bore a smile.
Kate Plested (16)

Papyrus
In darkness
I touch your safe, white surface -
Cold lover.
I feel you
Etch myself into your skin.
You absorb me -
Your silent tongue
Tastes all I am
Holds me in your mouth
Swallows pain.
In the dark quiet
I choose to tell you everything
You keep my secrets
Papyrus, sweet
Locked in your paper-thin heart.
Denise Eustace

Two-Party System
VAT on fuel and sewage in your water supply.
This is the Tories' thorn.

Union anarchy and left-wing extremism -
This could be your socialism.

Permanent unemployment and a health care system
that can't afford to care - but the
Conservatives keep on winning.

Public ownership - with all the doors closed -
and a useless rates system - no wonder
Labour sit on the Opposition bench.

A poll tax that erupts in riots and
a failed education that costs
the tax payer billions - more Tory cons.

Corrupt Labour councils that just can't deliver
and a rise in taxes that will make you shudder.

While your reading their manifestos -
a fat businessman is murdering a fox
and another is doing it with a teenage whore.
Matthew Lee

Monsieur Beige

My name is simply Monsieur Beige.
Beige by nature, beige by age.
As I stand and wait at Amersham station,
The girls look up to me with adoration.
    In rain, shine, sleet or snow,
    I dress in beige from head to toe.
    Pacing the ground to Baker Street,
    My beige torso sways to the beat.
But I'm just a lonesome and ordinary guy,
As the beigy days and trains go by.
My BBC friend says I'll be a star,
So no more trains but a luxury car.
    I must be the beige and the certain flair,
    From my tall machoness and carroty hair.
    In my Burberry coat and beige tweed cap,
    I'm really quite a dashing chap.

So if you need an escort or a model for the day,
Then I'll be at your service for a small price to pay.
For when I strike lucky and my ship sets sail,
Remember Monsieur Beige aboard the British Rail.
Penny Moore

Senility
To the old, time is no longer
A friend -
She comes to rend.
Arriving with destructive hands
She nears.
Snatching away the consoling gifts
Of mellowing years,
Wisdom, gentleness of mind,
The face wrinkled kind
Has now an emptiness - before not seen,
Making strange where once familiar had been.
Marion Caragounis

Job Application
A glass box of communication
Hides personality and fears,
Hope is desperate
As the last tokens of respectability
Drop into the machine.

Hand held smutting newsprint
Holds a chance of life
As ringing stops
A disembodied voice fills the space
With enquiry - Who?

A question of personal identity
Hangs in the air
Who am I?
That once was a holder of dreams
But no more.

A seeker of continuing existence
held in abeyance
By redundancy
Desperate to have a vacuum filled
With position

Face muscles ache as teeth unclench
To speak only
A few words
'Is the position advertised still free?'
Sorry vacancy filled!
Julie Carter

Those Words

They lie together with the mutual belief that the other is sleeping
Their bodies curve together naturally
He whispers those words
She laughs in disbelief
The silence of understanding is broken
The words lost
They smile in embarrassment
She feels him breathe and dare not move
He feels her heart and dare not speak
They're afraid
Each alone beside a stranger.
Kate D'Arcy-Evans

Child of War

The child, wide-eyed and wondering,
Dying before she has even lived;
Trapped behind bars, her world is one white room -
She will never know what it is to be loved.

And God, if you are listening,
Try to help us please:
Take away the pain of war,
of famine and disease.

The cot is bare, the mattress scrubbed,
The child is carried to her grave;
Her clothes are soaked and sterilized,
Then used again, and used again.

Dear God, if you are listening,
Why was she born at all?
How can you watch the misery,
The fate of one so small?

Two more brown eyes stare through the bars -
A tiny body in greying clothes;
She does not reach out to be held,
She reaches out for you.

And God, if you are listening
How can you stand and stare?
So many have been wondering,
If you are really there . . .
Gaelyn Jolliffe

The Hollyhock Clock
The Hollyhock Clock
Keeps a slow, slow time,
Moves up one flower each week.

It's seven feet high
And a dark, dark red,
So dark that it's almost black.

It stands before
An old, old wall,
Of flint and crumbling brick.

A white Montana
With a sweet, sweet smell,
Hangs heavy on that wall;

And through its leaves
And the white, white flowers,
The Hollyhock Clock keeps time.

It's October now
With cold, cold nights,
There's one last bloom in bud;

The very last flower
Of the long, long year -
The Hollyhock Clock runs down.
J S M Petterson

Harmony
I could find harmony
I hear it in my musical moods
I could reach through and touch
a moment, a single caress

I could hold harmony
for it penetrates my shield
a moment, in my heart

I could breathe harmony
filtered through the soiled air
for a moment, reawakening

I can see harmony
resting in the next field
I could reach, if I dare
but I'll wait -
for it to find me.
Julie-ann Woods

Untitled

Walking through the field of snow
I chanced to glance at the sunset glow
The sky was clear, a delight to behold
The sun in its glory, like a crock of gold.
At that moment, I paused to stare
Admiring nature, with time to spare
If only I could paint that scene
Of beauty, joy, and heavenly serene
Such pleasure I'd give to the busy few
Who find no time to stand and view.
Ruth Lelyveld

Old Woman 1985

I must not interfere, I must *not* interfere
except to sweep the floors, clean the bogs
wash the dishes, do the cooking, scour the sinks
and be thankful.

Yes, yes, I must do all the work and be *glad.*
I must at all times be respectful, and keep the peace
I must not complain, I must kerb all flaws of
personality - after all, do I really *need* one?

I must not be ill, or I will be punished.

I am lucky to be sixty-five and still able to work,
I cannot retire, I must be grateful.

Young woman - learn your catechism, and pray
for your salvation.
Amen.
Winnie Martin

Cavaliers Upon the Brow

Sheep Street was my childhood home,
cutting through fields of daisy foam.
Sheep Street was my childhood love,
where Scots pine towered high above,
where Winslow Hall stood high and wide
and my ancestors lived with pride,
where horses trotted in days long past
and traffic now goes much too fast,
where old houses shake and bits drop down.
Juggernauts rule my sad old town.
Shopkeepers used to wear aprons long,
now they and all the shops have gone.
Estate agents bought the grocer's shop.
When will this progress ever stop?
Fields of green gave way to tar;
then came the noisy motorcar
to houses built like boxes square
for townies to enjoy country air.
Sheep Street sees no drovers now,
only *Cavaliers* upon the brow.

Robert Cook

Nightfall

(Dedicated to my husband Tony)

Alone, in my little room, I think of you
At nightfall.
I sit and watch the passers-by
In daylight hours
And see the rain-lashed elder dip her bowers,
But only thoughts of you, my lost love, haunt me
At nightfall.
Dreams of bygone days return again and again
But sweet reminiscence and twilight memories
Are all in vain,
For you will never return, my lost love
At nightfall.

In my solitude and long, lonely hours
At nightfall,
I pray to the Lord above,
Let me not outstay
My time on earth, in heartbreak's pay,
For where you are, my love, I long to be
At nightfall.
The severed link when two were as one
Is harder to bear when
The long, long day is done.
But, dearest, I will always be with you
At nightfall.
Julia Eva Yeardye

The Lace Maker
She sits on the stool,
With downcast head,
Her gaze on the pillow
Plying bobbins and thread.

With age worn fingers,
Serene is her face,
Delicate the tracery,
Exquisite the lace.

What are her thoughts
As she sits there?
With a smile on her lips,
With a gift so rare.

What wisdom, what beauty,
Within that grey head?
Sweet gentle old lady
Plying bobbins and thread.
Etheldreda F E Nutt

The Late, Late Lullaby

The alarm clock has slept more than I have tonight.
It has been ticking in its sleep.
Quartz clocks do not need to tick.
They do it in their sleep
When they are dreaming of being real
Of what life was like in their grandfather's time
When people awakened unalarmed
Having been ticked for, and to, and to, and for,
To and fro throughout the night.

Hilary Mason

Confraternity

Pastor Pers-picacity,
A man of some tenacity,
Had a large capacity,
For drinking lots of gin.

Bishop Evan-gelical,
Discussing matters clerical,
Almost went hysterical,
When, Pers, he staggered in.

Canon Phil-ozophize,
Then began to sermonise,
That dear old Pers, must realise,
The error of his ways.

Reverend E-volution,
Proposed a resolution,
There must be a solution,
To better Pers' days.

Rabbi Ben-ediction,
Prayed with great conviction,
For Pers' long addiction,
To spirits on the shelf.

Moderator Tam-o'-shanter,
Listened to the banter,
Then opened a decanter,
And had a dram himself!
P F Whitlock

Delights of Life
I love to see a new day dawn,
And wake up to a nice, bright morn,
I love to see the stately trees,
When they are wafted by a gentle breeze.
I love to see the flowers grow,
How they get their colours, I do not know?
I love to see a little stream,
Meandering along, as if in a dream,
I love to see the children play,
And watch them skipping along the way,
I love to see the birds fly high,
And watch them soar up to the sky.
I love to see when it's time for bed,
The pillow where I lay my head.
Patricia Dinelli

The Old Lace Chest
(Thoughts on a gift from the granddaughter of a Wellingborough lace maker to the author)
Will it disintegrate, fade at a breath,
Like snow crystals fashioned in air,
That in wanton abandon are drawn to their death
As they kiss the warm windowpane there?

The spider's frost etchings hung out on the hedge
Are shattered by foraging thrush;
Could *this* beauty as swiftly be brushed to a shred
As that poor spider's rag in the bush?

Could it drift from my hand on a westering breeze,
Like seedlings of dandelion clock;
Or as delicate froth-caps on murderous seas
Be as easily rent by a rock?

These laces, so frail, seem as wraiths in a dream,
Woodbine and roses and fragrant bean flower;
Butterflies' wings and meandering stream,
Gossamer weblets from some elfin bower -

The crown and the tulip, Saint Catherine's wheel,
Fat bees, and the knot and the bell;
Forget-me-not, lily, and Solomon's seal -
All woven with consummate skill.

With pattern and pillow and bobbins and pins,
By dawning and noontide and candlelight's gleam.
But beauty was mocked by the age of machines,
Thus wilting the flower of the weaver of dreams.

High in a dark attic corner, we came
On the old oaken chest by a wall,
And brushing the dust from the lid, found a name -
Sarah Whitbread it read, that was all.
Joyce E Palmer

The Beggar
I've worked my fingers to the bone
For each penny that I own.
I am very proud to see
That I need no-one but me.

Every crust that I eat
I found lying at my feet.
Such was greed of someone's soul
They would not place it in my bowl.

Oh, I knock upon each door.
Such is life for people poor.
Then I work myself half dead
For a simple slice of bread.

And that bread is my one meal!
Oh! The hunger that I feel!
And my thirst torments me so!
I feel that life is my foe!

'Oh, hello, do come in,' they said.
Their faces said, 'Leave,' instead.
So on the doorstep I did stand
Holding out my bleeding hand.

I beg for food on bended knees.
'I'd like a little food, sir, please.'
He tells me just to go away.
I can do nothing but obey.

I have a stabbing pain to hide
And all my tears must be denied.
As man is cruel, cruel I must be
And mock all those worse-off than me.
Louise Fleet

Fireside Reflections
Winter was dressed in her silvery best,
Of frost, fog, and all the rest
that makes us huddle around the fire,
contemplating our desire
for warmer climes and sunlit beaches,
local vin and fresh, ripe peaches.
Winter in her finery,
helped my fireside reverie.
Ronald Leonard Draper

Untitled

I wait to grasp the man with the transparent stare
Who looks at me with tainted eyes
And as I smile he looks away to pretend he doesn't care

I walk into the evening shade and watch the human affair
You look at me with no surprise
And bark bitching for the creatures to drive me away to their lair.

You look through the walls as they rape the stones
And the panthers rip open my meat for the feast
I lay as the pig on the table as you condone
My bloody head in the cauldron of love though I am not a beast

The sirens warned what happened when you delve into a stranger's compassion
We have all seen and screamed as he gorged out your eyes
For the cast to spellbind the horror of young children
Playing with the orphaned wolves of pornography
Though we do not warn only lecture when the deed has happened
And the God has been pleasured
For thy is the kingdom of power and glory.
Karen Anne Rogers

Show Me the Prison

Keep out of the way; this man means trouble.
You see it in the manner his eyes twitch
and his hands pummel and torment the air
as none who is quite sane.

Here he is talking to himself at the bus depot;
on the floor with screwed-up wrappers
and the cigarette butts and the drained can of cola,
still muttering under his breath he will bed down.

Neurosis has all kinds of entries.
Look back twenty years, where the mind incessantly
attacks the same piece of glass like a trapped blue-fly.
Could I have been that man?
Merryn Williams

Roses for Anne
(Anne Tibble d. August 31st 1980)
Her roses still rampage over the fence
the door she would not lock is shut fast now
snowdrop, primrose, rose will bud again:
years of season into death for her.

> She fled space-age technology
> sent back the hired TV
> watched instead the warted toad
> stringing black pearls of life
> listened to black thief birds
> singing their ecstasy
> danced with mind and body to the poetry of Clare;
> her words ran with her into the morning
> rose with flocks of plovers
> sang with larks up under the sun
> delved with her own dark selves
> into the night's despair.

To this golden woman dancing in yellow dress
indelible on memory, honoured now in death
I bring these anniversary roses
wrapped in words of gentleness.
Mary Atterbury

First Snowfall
There's an unfamiliar mantle on the garden here today,
Obliterating all familiar joys:
No cherub smiling up at me, no brave new shoots to see,
No definition, movement . . . and no noise.

Is that the tub where once the gentians bloomed that glorious blue?
Will they survive, and blaze again next year?
And can that be the bush that had the bud all ready to burst?
I only pray you do not die, my dear.

The lilac buds are hidden, the urn is like a Christmas cake,
Like jewelled lace mantillas are the trees:
The fields all kiss the sky, and the sky embraces all,
And I'm all but moved to get down on my knees.

For this is nature speaking from a wise and perfect force,
Giving to all and everything its due:
There's strength and beauty for the souls of those who've eyes to see,
So in humility I say, 'Thank you.'
Kathleen Pateman

Teenage Trauma
A teenager's life is not all honey
They often have spots - and they never have money.
They spend hours in the bathroom, nearly all day
Using up all the deodorants, gels and hairspray.
Their music is always on, the volume really high
And they won't turn it down, no matter how loud you sigh.
They are constantly chatting on the phone
And are always asking Mum and Dad for a loan.

They borrow the car without a care
Do they think that it runs on fresh air?
They arrive home late, they never hurry
And don't realise how much their parents worry.
The house seems crowded with their friends
They try and keep up with fashion trends.
The jeans they wear are tatty and torn
Or they borrow new clothes that you've not yet worn.

They treat your home like a hotel
Living with teenagers can be hell!
If they are quiet - they're in a mood.
When visitors come, they are often rude
But as time passes, they'll settle down
So wear a smile instead of a frown.
Try and relax it's just a phase
Think back to your own teenage days.
Barbara A Wheatley

The Growing Grain

Indifferent to politics
The growing grain strives upwards.
Green and lush it knows
One thing.

Arms spending, balance of
payments,
Third world hunger,
set-aside
Mean nothing.

The roots delve strong
For hold and water.
Slender leaves
Draw in the light.

Against eroding soil,
Pollution, acid rain
And radiation
The growing grain
Has only one response.

The growing grain
Strives upwards.
Living to the full.

Ian Wilson

Encounters
(Prompted by Seigfried Sassoon's account of his journey from the Somme to Craiglockhart Hospital and his meeting there with Wilfred Owen)

This Day of Armistice I chanced upon a volume,
old and torn, of Seigfried's journey,
he Sir-named Sassoon of Somme

and Sorcerer's power to unshroud screams,
loose fury, blood, resuscitate
dead stares. I cowered

and grasped with him the lancing bullet
blighty-marked; to mourn with him the hideous
waste; to press with him the General-sense;

Dear Sirs, I do protest! This war
begun in liberation has turned to conquest.
I will not fight. I seek arrest.

Craiglockhart Rest Home for the newly mad
supplied the strangest meeting yet;
a youth in passioned phrases preaching life
rehearsed an anthem for his early death.

Returning - I met my own youth face
to face. Surely, I pressed, at this eleventh hour
you should not sleep.
Why not? she moaned. And burrowed deep.
Jennie Powell

Natural Blindness
How many people saw the rainbow,
Spawned in the teeth of the squall?
Not many - I'll warrant, at five-fifteen . . .
Locked in their cars . . .
Stuck in a traffic jam.

How many people saw the Kingfisher,
Breasting the corkscrew wind?
Precisely none - I'll have you know . . .
Eyes glued to *the box* at five forty-five . . .
For I was the only one!
Roger Wiggins

Operano

On acquiring the very first note -
A murmur of red blood lips
Shockingly awake amid the fear of silence.
Deep within a voice arose;
Bowels of the soul lifting.
Hands now grasping, lips in chase,
Blood bubbling to temptation.
Ecstatic! The orchestra begins.
Fighting, regaining strength:
stomach muscles building.
Supremously, each note, each word -
Slight echo of Omega.
Couraging bitter war;
Enchanting emotion with serene.
Alone, voice and instruments peaked harmony,
Resting in the light.
Making love exquisitely
To end a perfect night!

Julie Wills

Time Standing Still

He stares -
She's there,
Although they're
Both with
Someone else,
They are reaching
Into each other's
Bodies and minds.

She knows he's
Not just another
Part of her heart.
She's mesmerised,
His dark penetrating
Eyes set into her
Broken mind.
He won't allow
Her to leave
Their past behind;
Love is not blind,
It's just not kind.
Michelle Pettifer

Hellen and One
Alone in the old and new house
To me, like a mouse
Dumb to the spheres, what had I heard?
What was it I stirred?

I heard the wind above the fire,
The telegraph wire
Nodded; the brown side light was strained,
And the air was maned.

It tried to come in and damage,
The garden's rampage
Gasped; and then, as a clock struck one,
And a silent one,

Hellen and one, what I heard then
Was time, after men;
Our future, wordless like the air,
And there and not there.
Hugh Allott

Two's Company

You posed by a pool in the Costa Del Sol
I imagined you dressed like a gangster's moll
In scarlet and green

Your lipstick was smeared on a cigarette end
and your partner-in-crime with money to spend
stood by looking mean

My daydream took flight when you walked to the bar
Where the waiter was shining a glass like a star
But his eyes were on you

They were taking you in opportunity wise
As they searched for a promising look in your eyes
Pure Amethyst blue

In his day he had been a seducer-in-chief
When your mother last heaved a sigh of relief
In July sixty-nine

He mixed you a drink so nicer than nice
It poured long and cool over cherries and ice
Sparkling like wine

You walked back my way and threw me a glance
I caught it first time but surprised at the chance
Knocked over my beer

Funny how you got under my skin
We'll go there again when the money rolls in
Maybe next year.

J D MacLennan

Buckinghamshire
Remaining so Forever . . .

To think of other places
with all their cars and noise,
The peacefulness of Buckinghamshire
brings, oh so many joys;

The gentle rolling of the hills
the land so ripe and green,
The cattle grazing in the fields
the air so fresh and clean;

The rivers that meander past
the woodland over yonder,
The pace of life, much slower
with time to sit and ponder;

The feeling of *Community*
that here still lingers on
when in so many other towns
this value's long since gone;

The butcher or the newsagent
will stop to say, 'Hello.'
The people passed along the street
are people that you know;

To be blessed with such beauty
we each must now endeavour
To keep our county special
remaining so, forever.
Tanya Burgess

Desert

The land stretches before me
On for miles around
Can you see the ending
Of this dry and dusty ground?

It has a majestic beauty
The loneliness of true peace
Reaching on to the horizon
Where existing worlds cease
As far as the eye can see
The desolate earth lies bare
Undulating windswept mountains
melting distance layer by layer
Without a cloud in the sky
The sun sweeps this desolate
Where lost souls wander still
Cast from the hand of fate
As darkness lays its velvet cloak
Surrounding features fade
With the cool kiss of night
Daylight fears are swept away
Facing out over this deserted land
At my back, the world I despise
I ask forgiveness for all I've done
And the courage to survive.
Carol Moore

Gifts

Today my colleagues said 'Goodbye' to me,
I'd known them all for over thirty years,
They gave me presents in the factory
As I held back the many waiting tears,
I took their gifts, a silver Parker pen,
A golf bag, and a card with their names for
Which I truly thanked each one and then
I turned and walked out through the exit door.

Maybe some day I'll see them in the pub,
Or street, they'll say, 'Hello,' then, 'Sorry got
To go old man;' I'll miss the daily hub
Of talk and news at work and such a lot
Of things; I've got the gifts they kindly gave,
But still I'm one step nearer to the grave.

Jack Tapley

Dying Creation

Children lying
Dead on the street
Innocent people dying
Getting shot, getting beat
Trodden underfoot
Ground to a pulp
By armies of soldiers
Soldiers looking for hope
Hope for their countries
For a better place
But what place is there
With no human race?
In the eyes of the world
The problem's not there
(It'll disappear if they leave it alone)
If they show they don't care.
But no summit conference
Will solve the dilemma
It's action we need
Not just now but forever . . .

Jo Howson

Contradictory Uncertainties

If the impossible were possible
you'd be here with me.

If the implausible were plausible
we two would both be free.

If the impractical were practical
we'd never have dreamt our dreams.

Or love's howitzers not have shattered
our lives into smithereens.
Now, across domesticity's no-man's land.

I see your tempting form,
but dare not cross the minefield,
or watch for tomorrow's dawn.
Dave Aldus

Blind Love
I did not want my heart to wake yet he woke it
And what for?
To speak so true and act as if I was not there.

He trampled blindly, oozing alcohol through every pore.
I was the spectre, obliterated by his vacant stare.

For some he had his senses.

I am as a child, tugging at his sleeve
His eyes are focused on them - never me.
His face averted from my plea.

To watch as his sated arms enfold another
As false fingers clutch her head to his benign balls
I am lonely and lost.

I shake inside and smile and shrug.
It's just the drink, they pacify me
Just the drink when I'm not there
When I'm not present to love or care - or witness . . .

He owes it (has said it) to abstain for others
Yet I can take it, this estrangement
I'm that type.
My allies gone and only the dawn attempts to hold me.

Seven hours
He hasn't known me
Blind ears and eyes are all that sympathise.

Is this norm
To be excluded and forsaken?
Hurt is prickling inside
How can the knowledge I now have hide.
Fay Clark

Lecture in the Apple Loft

The clock beats its way slowly
Through the monotony of the
Droning voice of one who calls himself
Teacher - that happy breed of
Knowledgeable men and women who
Enthusiastically impart their
Knowledge to the
Bored ears of students -
  Like a bumble bee
  Short-legged and rounded
  Belly, he irritates the ears
  As does a docile wasp
  In autumn.
Deborah Hearn

Libra

Witty and smart,
I read in the chart,
The signs of a Libra man,
If the party is dull,
Could he liven it up,
Yes, I'm sure he probably can.

If you ask him a question,
He won't answer you straight,
But if you walk up the pathway,
He'll open the gate,
He will butt in and tease you,
But he'll do you no harm,
'Cause he is a Libran and he's known for his charm.
Austin James Fenn

The Pawn
Screams of the new-born,
Fresh ground to sow,
Submission and obedience,
The seeds of control.

He'll be drained of his spirit,
Trained to be meek,
Clothed in his ignorance,
And fed our deceit.

Shackled by principles,
Content he is free,
The child grows to manhood,
But still cannot see.

Riddled with morals,
Under the thumb,
Left by a censored existence,
Intellectually numb.

He lives his life blinkered,
Our wishes, his goals,
He hands us his children,
Surrenders their souls.

A pawn in our power games,
Unwitting slave,
He'll swallow hypocrisy,
From cradle to grave.
Graham Gillam

Hilda
She walks with the same spring step
She is quite unchanged
Her hair still brown
Her face unlined.

Yet she seems quite different
Was I really so enchanted with her
- fifteen years ago.

First glimpsed across a new-mown field of hay
With the same quick step
The same colour hair
And the innocent face.

She seems the same
Is it I who is different now?
Or has the spinning world
And cruel passing time
Altered all
And made mock of us and our feelings.

She does not see me
I do not move
She passes
With her beautiful but impassive face.
I, in my puzzlement,
Two different people?
John W Dossett-Davies

The Rose
As morning broke on a clear dawn
A rosebud popped into bloom
With the dew glistening on its stem
A symbol of love in a world of gloom.
Ivor Wright

Untitled
Dawn! Heralding a new day, quiet sky,
Peaceful earth voices shrilled; bird cry.
Lazy sleepers, know you what you've missed?
Wait you for an hour sunkissed,
Sultry heat to weary you.

Dawn song! Birds competing with an aptitude
Cat chasing mouse in an age old feud
Life's sleeping, never saw the dawn creeping
Waiting for a clock to give a time
Missing out on all that is sublime.

Twilight! Heralding the moonlight, star bright
Slowly waning leaves, shadows creeping
Billowing clouds, with red glow seeping
Lovers walking hand in hand, hearts leaping
Sunlight corn, a sister to the dawn.
H G Perry

Hypothermia
We found her still and silent, in her chair
where ice-cold air froze the whispered horror on our lips.
Her shawl, a threadbare thing, had slipped
from her shoulders to the floor,
and, somewhere in the house, an unfed cat
was scratching at an unrelenting door.
And though completely without sight
her eyes still stared, in vain entreaty,
at the bare white bars of an uncoined fire,
grinning in derision of her plight.
It was a sight we would always remember,
or so we swore
when standing in that cold-store tomb,
yet, scarce had the womb of winter released the head
of spring, than already we were forgetting
December's bitter sting.
Mary L Wykes

There Is No Love

There is no love, so lovers say, that cannot touch each sense
For when such people meet, the body's wondrous magic shows
And in every way becomes the welcome prisoner
Held within the greatness of love's blessed spell.

There is no love that cannot be read in lovers' eyes
That tenderest look inspired by true heartfelt desire
Shows the surprise and wonder of each meaning glance
And shows so clear the slightest anguish magnified.

There is no love that does not quicken at the slightest sound
A sudden indrawn breath, a sigh, soft whispered words
Some sudden movement, imperceptible to most
The crossing of one leg upon another, the rustle of a dress.

There is no love that does not feel the slightest touch
Gentle fingertips against the skin, asking exploring, still,
Bodies soft movements, the trembling breathless contact made
Soft lips in homage, small token of an outward sign.

There is no love that can resist the body's subtle scent
Radiating a sense of near primeval source
Mixed with the mystic perfumes of oriental blond
Creating that deep excitement which only lovers know.

There is no love that cannot stay those words
The age old promises, endearments, so well refined
Caught on the brink of passions ageless art,
Yet always fresh, so full of youth and true.

There is no love that stops the final consummation
Completeness, a unity between two souls
Struggling against all reason to attain the final goal
Breaking as a million suns into unutterable bliss.

There is no love when doubt, uncertainty and fear creep in
For when lovers' question love their dreams begin to fade
And all the greatness of their lives is gone
They look, and lo, they find quite suddenly, there is no love.
Anthony E L Cook

A Friend
Possessing there,
A mind so complex,
Yet knowable to me,
In all its variable moods.

Always there,
To understand feelings unspoken,
Knowing what to say,
And how to say it.

Being there,
To hold my hand,
Bringing happy, carefree moments,
Lingering in spite of time.

Always there,
Easy and yet intricate,
Temper like a storm,
Raging a quiet war within.

Being there,
Sharing laughter and discussion,
To hold your own,
In a world unknown.

Always there,
Not alone but surrounded,
By people who care,
To see friendship and love.
Juliette Ireland

Forgotten Graves

Where headstones bow on forgotten graves
Where moss and weeds envelope stone
Where yew trees sway on windswept days
Mourners pray over rotting bones.

Storm clouds over the churchyard breaking to blue
Throws shade on flowers from the sun in the east
shiny marble monolith upright and true
stirring past memories resting in peace.

Footsteps over churchyard gravel
In time with tolling bells
beats a path the soul to travel
beyond their empty shells.

Brass will tarnish, wood will rot
deep down within the earthy hole
compressed beneath these chosen plots
long forgotten souls.

When tears have dried for the dearly deceased
When the ground is hard as clay
When the door has closed on the funeral feast
We kiss the dust away.

Edward McErlane

Another Day in Life

First thing on a frosty morning,
Hope is high and the day is dawning,
Expectation in the air,
The sun is up, and none's the care.
Six o'clock and roof top glistens,
Cuckoo calls as hillside listens,
Skylark adds its voice and sings
As another day in life begins.

In their houses, people stir,
Alarm clocks ring and engines purr.
Time to start the working day,
While big machines turn time away.
Eight o'clock, so off to school son,
Don't forget the golden rule, son.
Do the work and pass the test,
The system takes care of the rest.

Ten o'clock and sun gets hotter,
Drunken tramps in graveyard totter.
In the office, people writing,
On the dole queue, people fighting.
Frost has melted, hope has gone,
The new day didn't last for long.
The sun goes in, it starts to rain
On another day in life again.

Day is done, and night arrives,
It's resting time for nine to fives.
Tramps are sleeping in the park,
Seeking refuge from the dark.
Midnight now, and what's the score?
Today was like the day before,
And in the morning, nothing's new -
Just another day in life to do.
Richard Gordon

Under the Clock
I met her on a Friday night,
at a table in the street,
I gazed into her enchanting specs
and longed for our glasses to meet,
and clink together like champagne glasses
in a moonlit toast to new friends,
followed up by a sexy snog,
lips to lips,
lens to lens.

Danny Wilson

The Churchyard Clock

The churchyard clock chimed one o'clock
and told the busy throng,
that dinner time was halfway through
and please don't be too long.
Weary mothers hurry home
to prepare the evening tea.
Businessmen in pinstriped suits
so full of jollity.
But then there's lovers just like us
that wish the time stood still,
to be together on our own
with dreams enough to fill.
Then everyone rushed back to where
they came before the chime
had struck to tell the busy hordes
that now it was the time,
that parting lovers kiss and hug
and say a fond farewell.
The chime announced that dinner time
had spoilt that magic spell.

Eric O White

Hot Earth

The colour of summer is born in the wheat
That's ripened to gold in the shimmering heat;
A promise of plenty that patterns the weald,
Emblazoned with poppies aflame in the fields.
And dotted with crimson the strawberry teas
Are served in the shade of the sheltered trees
that filter the rays to the grass at our feet
And dapple our hands with gold as we eat.
Crowds congregate round the festival flowers
Drowsy heads nodding away fragrant hours.
Dark days are dimmed as the landscape unfolds
And colours the canvas in crimson and gold.

K J Pettit

Rap Song for the Earth

OK bro, I'm talking about the planet
Destruction ain't cool - we really oughta ban it.
OK sis, I'm talking 'bout the greedy
They just gotta grab - they forget the needy.
They're croppin', loppin', choppin' down the trees
Burning out the sky with CFCs
Givin' us cancers, pollutin' the seas
And when they done all that they ask for fat fees.
They got an attitude problem - think they're smart
But it just ain't clever to rip out the world's heart.
Some day soon they better do something quick
'Cos when the earth gets sick we all get sick.
We gotta stop tippin', strippin', rippin' the earth
Gotta think about slowin' rates of birth
Gotta get nature back to purity
Gotta work together - I'm talkin' unity.
OK kids get with the funk
Do what you can to recycle junk
'Cos we gotta recycle to save resources
Gotta get together and all join forces.
Yo! We gotta realise what the planet's worth
Gotta do our bit to save the earth.
And so I say you gotta make the distinction
Between carin' for the world or facin' extinction.
Fay Dickinson

Curriculum Vitae

Lying in bed, I make up another CV,
Applications are my employment,
I'm work shy, me.
Name,
Date of birth,
Address,
These are the only things I've got to impress.

Education,
Qualifications,
Passed me by
I'm a professional job seeker,
Two words; work shy.

Work history,
I've no history to tell
I haven't work ethics in any blood cell.

References,
That's a joke!
They'd say, 'He's a lazy, unsocial so and so;
That Bloke!'

I want to be a footballer, doctor or astronaut,
But I don't like space, medicine or sport.
I can turn my hand to any trade; I'm very versatile
But if you offered me employment, 'I'd run a mile.'

Another CV to send off, but I don't know why,
Thanks for your time.
Yours faithfully,
Mr Work Shy.

Robert Howgate

Just a Thought

I hate to cut the roses back,
Just when they're full of bloom,
Then put the cuttings in a sack,
To give the new growth room.

It seems that faithful service given,
And joy, are all for nought,
If I can cast away these things
Without a wistful thought.

It may be when I'm very old,
(Much older than today)
The world may find its heart too cold
To feel that I might stay.

I could be still with agile mind,
But stiffening in the limb,
Someone will say, 'Just to be kind,
We'll make an end of him.'
Roy William Blenco

My Children
My children. Eyes flawless blue and seeing all.
You are mine. Have I the wherewithal
to hold you, keep you, succour you?
I am growing still, my learning not yet through.
My children. My heart leaps with your being.
It is myself in you that I am seeing.
A part of me, in eye and hair and finger.
My heritage where those who went before still linger.
Yet separate. And as you now take up your role
You are a part. But also whole.
Exquisite pain you cause me, tiny things.
I am a pendulum. Eternal swings.
Emotions tugging at my soul and mind.
We are my life! And still I look behind
To wonder at my days before. And what it was
That made me open wide the door.
To let you enter and mayhem my world
With tiny, silk soft, iron fingers curled
Around my heart. And yet.
You are the nearest thing to heaven I can get.
You trusting, crying, laughing ones.
Your nature warmer and more brighter than the sun.
We are entwined forever in life's chance.
My children. Trust in love. And dance!.
Donna Hughes

Future Euphoria

As we wallow in the mire of humanity
That has come to be our world.
Blind through greed, such insanity.
The sacred secret is unfurled.
Beyond this life of shallow pleasure
Lies a future of love on earth.
Peace will be a common measure,
No longer buried in the dirt.
The struggle to find the real reasons
As to why we live or die
Shall become clearer than the seasons.
Who will need to weep or cry?
At one with ourselves.
Likewise God and man.
Selfish needs eternally shelved
As we strive to give all we can.
Euphoria will be felt throughout the land.
Years of life more numerous than grains of sand.
Euphoria awaits in God's mighty hand.
Paul French

Joys of the Tide

On sun-drenched beaches - children shriek,
A wave of excitement flows.
The tide, with whisper - creeps to a peak,
Turns with a hiss - tickling wriggling toes.

Peals of laughter tinge the air -
As sparkling waters splash,
And children dash from everywhere,
Jumping white frothy foams as they crash.

Mums and dads, with babes in arms,
Gasp merrily, as they run to greet -
The swirling tide with all her charms,
Sliding slippery sand, from under their feet.

The sun, as wanting to join the fun,
Shines happily with pride.
Ecstatic bodies romp and run.
Such are the joys of the tide!
Valerie Harris

Time
Time is oblivious,
It passes regardless of emotion,
We are powerless.
It will flow, even when we die.
Time can't be grasped,
Nor seen,
Nor heard,
Relentless in its pursuit of the unknown,
To the darkness after the light.
Time is a path,
Taken, because we have no choice.
Christina Urso-Cale

Jack
A long-haired man so thin and gaunt,
Comes bounding over fences.
In the quiet just before dawn,
He moves in the shadows
Your eyes saw something there.
Then you hear the manic laughter
Now your mind senses fear.
He is the darkened character
From all the children's tales,
Those thoughts that made you shiver
The tales that chilled your bones
And now you feel like seven
When Jack comes passing by
You're fumbling for the lightswitch
But this is no dream tonight.
Robert Mead

The Digger

On a cold and damp September morn',
A baby cries another born,
The wind blows softly through the trees,
Dewdrops glisten on the leaves,
A raven casts a gazeful eye,
On village people passing by,
And down below he sees old Fred,
Working on the ground where he was wed,
He's in the graveyard all alone,
Surrounded by markers made of stone,
In a six-foot hole he toils the earth,
Shovelling soil for all he's worth,
Another hole, another day,
Another poor soul, passed away.

S J Newman

A Chinese Garden

I will make a tranquil Chinese garden,
Like the sentient men of old;
A place for silent contemplation,
for deeper meditation:
A place for the nativity
of new created thought.

There will be no painful, mental anguish
Thinking when and what to plant:
The times of temporary frustration:
of difficult selection:
The times of no felicity
with which my life is fraught.

And in that tranquil, Chinese garden
I will gaze like men of old:
See light on white-holed masonry,
on the leaf-made tracery:
See shade on each declivity
where sunshine can't be caught.

Lilian Butler

The Two Junior Hustlers

The two junior hustlers
Chalk their custom made cues
In the empty pool room,
Listening to a jukebox
That plays only for girls,
Waiting for male opponents
That never turn up.
They yawn
And pull on college scarves
Leaving
Into a drizzling
Midlands night
Devoid of men.

Paul Wilkins

Things That Go Bump in the Knight

Sir Windbag, a knight from Kirkcudbright,
Owned stables of stallions and mares.
One day, after racing at Newbury,
The poor man was caught unawares.

He'd managed to bring home a winner,
A filly called *Succulent Peach,*
And as guest at the evening dinner
He was asked to deliver a speech.

The menu and wine list were splendid,
Which tempted Sir Windbag to eat
Till his innards were hugely distended,
And he couldn't get out of his seat.

As beans began blasting the turkey
The vodka took aim at the gin.
Our knight was a piggy un-perky,
His speech-making talent grown thin.

With garlic fumes gassing the trifle,
His waistband grew tight as a drum.
No more was he able to stifle
The carnage inside his poor tum.

The scampi had slaughtered the salmon:
The Riesling had ruined the roast.
He wished he'd had less of the gammon,
As he couldn't stand up for the toast.

His audience sat there dumbfounded
To hear his embarrassing plight,
As the banqueting chamber resounded
To things going bump in the knight.
Roger Langdon-Davies

Looking Upward
You are bound to look at the trees
In bud each year,
What does it mean to you
Does it open up the mind
and bring forth in a flood
Memories of the past?
The leaves come alive once more
Waving in the breeze,
They are telling us again
That what looks dead springs forth
Once more in infinite majesty.
So when we discard this frame of ours
No matter when it be,
May we be clothed in garments rare
Fit for eternity.
Joan E Cook

Didn't I Always

Didn't I always say, that one of the nice
things about being married, was
having someone to cuddle up to in bed.
Now the bed is too big and so cold.
Didn't I always like to see you,
sitting in your own armchair by the fire,
smiling into my face, making the whole
room feel warm, cheerful and secure.
Now your empty chair makes me afraid in
a cold bleak world.
And didn't I always like to feel your hand
holding mine, as we walked down the street,
We didn't mind the rain in our faces, or the
cold nip of frost in the air, we were happy.
Now there is no soft touch, nothing to hold
but the shopping bag, nothing to feel but
the harsh reality that I am alone.
Didn't I always wish, that when the time
came, we could still be together,
Oh my dear, didn't I, always.

Elizabeth Bell

Untitled

You have no right
to call me
a poet . . . because
I am not,
neither am I a
dreamer.

I am just me,
lost in this silence . . .
betrayed by
my longing desire of
being.

Marco A Reale

On the Spot

I stood on this land
Where I was born,
I have not seen it for many a year
The old die, babies are born and take their place.
Like everything,
So you make sure
That you don't leave it too late.

Lancelle McKnight

Conflict

Two forces pulling different ways,
Fighting that goes on for days,
Each side has different views,
Now's the time for you to choose,
Who is wrong and who is right?
Why do people have to fight?

There are places out of bounds,
Soldiers falling to the ground,
Muddy bloody wet and cold,
Only doing what they're told,
Soldiers left where they lie,
Why do people have to die?

Are the leaders really wise?
Or is war based on many lies?
So many injured, so many lost,
Can anyone really count the cost?
All is over all is done,
Has anybody really won?

Bobbie Scrivener (12)

The Human Zoo

I look at the others trapped in the zoo
Sleeping, fighting, playing
They look so fine but please don't touch
Look nice to hold but hurt too much.

Walk from their cage and into mine
But there's no key, no bars, this time
There's no outside to stare into
And you can't touch the ones who hurt.

So work pays for your concrete pleasure
A window to regret and question at leisure
Cage yourself to escape the outside
But who can run when everyone hides.

Alive - so alive - and far too aware
In a world full of animals, disabled by despair
Do you ever think to yourself
If only they couldn't talk
If only their traps weren't there!

Shelley Sandeman

A Real World and Doubting Mind

(For poet John Clare)

Alcoved at All Saints
He watches the beer cans roll
And the nearest he gets to the country is birdshit.

Has he sat through the centuries
Marooned
Cocooned
At St Andrew's? And do we call him mad
Because he shouts, 'Betrayal!'

Upon occasion, as one would -
Watching one's birds and woods
Diminish?
Finish
The job: Stop up the mouth with litter

That wails for Mary and knows not what he is,
Or if God knows
God-knows.

Love, human love is what there is
And all there is.
Nor Gods nor fields survive
That 'Foreign country called the past'
Though civic celebrations
Seek the lie Northamptonshire
Is still
By competitive will,
Greater than asphalt.

Old man - you'll write
No more;
No more shall we that know
No more than what you tried to teach us,
Thrill to Patty, Byron or Trotty Wagtail:

But if we read not, heed not,
The addictive rhymester,
Beloved lunatic
Will see only the waste in the wasteland
The filth in the field,
And in the pollute stream
Soggy pages of John Clare's dream
Not bream.
Barry L Hillman

The Devil's Punchbowl
We were in love in 1938
The Devil's Punchbowl beckoned,
we succumbed.
The purple heather blazed, contrasted with
The glory of the setting sun, blood-red
with magic rays.

We are still in love in 1994
The Devil's Punchbowl's changed,
The purple heather's gone, replaced by
woodland grove,
The blood-red sun cannot get through,
The magic stays.
Dolly Harmer

Buachaille Etive Mor
Cliffs of Crystal Night
As black and cold as Fear
Leap up from Rannoch Moor,
Slicing the pristine air

The azure moorland sky
Defines His perfect cone
His slopes are sheer and vast,
A Desert born of stone.

No lifeless mountain this,
He watches and He waits;
An Angel raised from Hell
Guards Glen Coe's ancient gates.

What Demon shaped those crags,
This mountain filled with Dread;
Whose evening summit snows
Glow sinister and red?

All travellers through the Glen
Must stop and stare in Awe,
The sight of Him enough
To thrill men to the core.

A Sentinel of Dark,
His task is without end;
While Ages come and go
This lonely post He'll tend.

Great Herdsman of Etive,
Your cold unmoving eyes
Will stare out on these moors
Down the silent centuries.
Angela Kelly

The Abnormality of Compassionate Man
Normality is in the eye of the beholder.
Attitudes aren't born - but are nurtured,
They flourish and bloom
And having achieved maturity
Are unwittingly lodged, deep,
Within the bigoted id of mankind.

Remember, when faced by an individual
Not conforming to your status quo,
Be it for physical or psychological reasons
Or for whatever reason,
The perception of normality adopted
Is mirrored in the minds of your peers.

So take time to look once again
Convey empathy, not pity, nor distaste.
As behind the psychosis, creed,
The colour or the body broken,
Is in essence you.
Philip Sowter

Memory Fragments

It's the frozen tongue on a snowfruit
From the *stop me and buy one* man,
The soap laden breath of a copper,
The aroma of stew from a pan.

It's a big black balloon descending,
To cover the whole of my face,
A very loud high pitched whistle
In my ears - then nothing - but space.

It's the heart stopping thrill of the *dipper*,
A hair band dropped in the *gods*,
My Dad going on his pub outing
And on Saturdays - studying *odds*.

It's the sound of *a Monastery Garden*,
Tortured by the *keys*,
It's the Sunday roast beef lunch
And the shrimps and winkles teas.

Spinning tops, hot dusty pavements
Covered in coloured chalk,
The peculiar smell of the classroom,
Where for hours we dared not talk.

Buttons and boots all gleaming,
At the end of the nightly task,
Tear gas - smarting, choking,
Ordeal without a mask.

The thrust of the bow through the water,
The blazing sun in the sky,
On the sea, the dancing sparkle,
And the myriad fish that fly . . .
Marjorie Empson

Crocodile

As I went out to Bejam's for a bag of frozen peas,
I found a dozen people crawling on their hands and knees.
I made polite enquiry for the reason they did that;
'We're looking for a reptile in a Dolly Varden hat,'
'A Dolly Varden hat?'
'A Dolly Varden hat. A dolichocephalic in a Dolly Varden hat.'
Joyce Rowland

Space

As far as we know at this point in time
We have no space neighbours we can define
Flying saucers and that UFO sighting
Could be connected with the prevailing lighting
Crop circles are another phenomenon
Supposedly related to a space companion
In the case of one or two of these
Homo Sapiens were simply trying to tease.

The origin of the universe has not been resolved
Although many researchers are presently involved
Working at a frantic pace
Exploring the limits of outer space
With infra red and radio telescope
They pick up signals with which they hope
Will give them the information they need to
Decide whether the Big Bang or Steady State is true.

Space probes such as Galileo
Hurtling through solar winds that blow
Are helping in our quest to find
Solutions to problems that boggle the mind
Due to the vastness of space
Unfortunately they cannot keep pace
With galaxies that are speeding away
A thousand times faster than they.
C N Hughes

Goodbye Eyes

By now I should be worldly-wise,
Yet the many things I wished I said
Evaporated in my head,
When I saw your goodbye eyes.

That moment took me by surprise,
The proper words just wouldn't come,
Emotion struck and I was dumb,
When I saw your goodbye eyes.

There are some things we can't disguise,
For something dies each time we part,
There was deep sorrow in my heart,
When I saw your goodbye eyes.

Life is full of *ifs* and *whys,*
Though I'll long recall your friendly greeting,
The lasting memory of our meeting,
Are those misty goodbye eyes.
John Leppard

Machu Picchu

Like myriad diamonds
tumbling in turmoil
over a bed of stone,
the river winds its way
'round mountains' slopes,
gnawing great gorges
over which the
Sun God reigned.
And the lost city
of granite was found,
high on the mountain's peak,
forever to thrill
and mystify man.
Lucinda Hearne

Zachran

I gaze upon your sleeping face
Such tranquillity lies there
I sigh, because as usual
Your hands are in your hair.

I untangle little fingers
But your grip, it holds me tight
Your lashes flutter gently, then
Eyes open, shining bright

I say, 'Sorry,' oh so softly
As I always do
And with my lips I brush your cheek
And whisper, 'I love you.'

A dimple's there lopsidedly
Your smile is not yet straight
'Hush little man,' I croon to you
'The time is very late.'

You whimper oh so quietly
As I stroke and pat a while
Your lids they flutter downwards
And I check, there is no smile.

Instead there is contentment
And I wonder what I've done
To deserve the love you give for free
In just knowing you're my son.

Robin Wilding

Love and Faith

This very moment, my emotions run deep,
These past eight years my father fell peacefully asleep,
Watching a programme of *Welsh male voice* choirs,
Listening intent, such inner feelings, inner desires.

All the wonderful music, all the powerful hymns,
My father so proud, how he loved to sing,
His face full of love, for his beloved Wales,
How I wish I had listened to his many tales.

Tales of passion, tales of woe,
Much depression in Wales, he knew he had to go,
Far away from the land he loved so much,
Taking his own family, soon to be out of touch.

Such courage needed, to leave loved ones behind,
Leaving one's family, not knowing what he will find,
Nowhere to live, no job, no home,
Simply love and faith, in God alone.

Once living in London, many years later I was born,
Company for my sister, life a struggle, parents forlorn,
Missing their heritage, way out of touch,
Parted from their families, they loved so much.

How I wish dear father, I had spent more time,
Letting you know how much I loved you, your devotion so fine,
Now you are gone, this moment does not seem real,
Too late to tell you, exactly, how I feel.
Laura

Early Morning
(For Laura)

The clouds drift on,
        Quite unimpressed
By that
        Half-moon,
Who in cerulean
        Awaits the dawn,
As I,
        Half-awake.

Even the blackbird
Has whistled
Only once -
Half-heartedly;
Aware, perhaps, of
The cat loping
In mere
Half-light.

Then gradual
Breaks the day,
As if
Half-unexpected;
And chestnut leaves
The breeze abandons,
Suddenly
Half-spent.

Now, no clouds ride
As you begin
To pale,
Half-moon.
To tinted glory
You can leave the world
And I,
To sleep.
Jim Finch

Changing Seasons
Trees stark
With the undress of their leaves
Standing still, tall to the sky
Changing colours
No movement now, silence
Autumn's here.

With the shredding of their leaves
Brown they change to golden
Birds in flight
Flock together, destination unknown.

Not a rustle
Not a sound
Trees stripped bare undressed to the sky
Leaves lie, carpet under foot
Colours brown and golden
Autumn's here, days changing fast
Dark and sombre now
Quietness still days
Calm
Trees asleep, resting
Come 'round spring.
Marjorie-Ann Warden

Buckinghamshire - Merely Centre Stage?
How many miles, the sea?
One hundred, maybe more?
Yet here, the setting sun is viewed
floating, sinking, crimson-hued;
bold as any seen from western shore.

No lesser feat as dawn's
emerging shades of light,
rising, spreading, all-embracing,
darkest night with day replacing,
touches all, as west with east unite.

How distant then, the sea?
No further than a glance.
Helen Harlow

The Sepia Print

Funny how little things can devastate. A word, a laugh,
Opening an old book, and life's perspective compresses.
It was earthquake for me, finding a mislaid photograph
Of summer children playing weddings. The girls, feeling smart
In their mums' hats and shoes, are prettier than princesses.
Clutching buttercup bouquet and reluctant groom, each wife
Poses; her glow of innocence, unseen then, wrenches the heart.
Which of them has survived sliding down the razor blade of life?

In their faces, the faith I can see in better tomorrows
Is destined to become nostalgia. Hope is a treacherous friend!
At this end of life's disappointments and sorrows,
As time has ticked the stars in their eyes to a wiser glint,
Are they, like me, trying to regain the art of pretend?
Where is my child-wife now, I wonder. For me, at last,
All that remains of her is this single postcard print:
A bookmark from the closed volume of the past.

Malcolm Wheatman

The Swan

A swan is beautiful as it glides along,
As white and pure as a young child's song,
Here today but gone tomorrow,
Never shows a sign of happiness or sorrow,
They float along in all their glory,
Just like it says in the fairy story,
They have no troubles as their minds are free,
Unlike people such as you and me,
They brighten up the river along with other ducks
and fish,
To speak their language would be my only wish,
Then they spread their wings and fly away,
And I know they will return again some day.

Jacey Kessler

In Your Absence

Carefully with serrated scissors and a steady hand
I cut you out of my favourite photograph
the family at play by a windswept Suffolk harbour
I managed just the right amount of background
Now you jostle for position on the pin board
with handy hints and leaflets that I've never thrown away.
You follow me around the room
Never faltering or passing judgement.
If you could hear me now
may I remind you twenty years
is a long time not to reappear.
Sometimes on a bad day
when the heart is bursting to embrace or tell of an
important detail I approach the board
turn the photograph upside down or turn it 'round
until the feeling's past.
Sometimes I've had to take you down *carefully*
and put you in the drawer.
One day the telephone will ring or a grey haired
man will slowly pass the window
looking for his daughter.
Wendy Breckon

The Squirrel

Ash tree branches bend and rustle.
Now the elders shake and shift.
Squirrel is on the prowl again.
Taking the hedgerow route to the garden
Leaving his hide-out to forage for food.
Aground and balanced on puissant hind legs,
He displays his magnificent tail
Silvery, furry, rich and silky
Like rippling sea against the setting sun.
Eyes search restlessly through four horizons,
Antennae ears scan constantly,
Front paws busy like divines at beads.

Still, yet not still - ever watchful.
A door slams. No time to linger.
Graceful tail becomes a rudder,
Flat against the rough tree bark.
Now the branches bend more fiercely,
Panic flight is heavier,
Noisier, faster . . .
Aloft, alone and in his sanctuary
Squirrel catches frightened breath.
The blackbird's nest is still secure.
Alan Murton